Juan Carlos Jim

Dialogue 2 dot 0

A tweet-book on social networks for managers and entrepreneurs

C O G R A F

Published by Cograf Inc.
June 2011

Dialogue 2 dot 0
A tweet-book on social networks
for managers and entrepreneurs
June 2011

Author: Juan Carlos Jimenez
Facebook: www.facebook.com/jucarjim
Twitter: @jucarjim

Published by Cograf Inc.
www.cografinc.com

ISBN-13: 978-1463556419

C O G R A F

Contents

Objectives of this tweet-book

This text is oriented to entrepreneurs, managers and executives in marketing, advertising, public relations or human resources.

Its content is for who want a better understanding of how to benefit from social networks to promote a project or organization.

Do you want to know more about Web 2.0 without being overwhelmed by a huge amount of technical information?

Are you looking for practical references that will help you establish a presence in social media without "killing yourself trying"?

As an entrepreneur, business owner, manager and communications professional, I ask myself these same questions.

I don't believe that opportunities just appear; you have to explore them, build them and cultivate them continuously.

Since 1994, I've explored Internet opportunities, and I must admit that I learned more when I shared what I already knew.

In this short book, I'm presenting you with the most important management ideas that I've come across related to social networks.

You won't find recommendations for specific software or technologies, but instead, just ideas that will help you come to your own conclusions.

This isn't a technical book and it won't tell you how to manage the technical aspects of social networks.

My goal is to provide you with strategic communications criteria that you should keep in mind when you use Facebook or Twitter.

I'll give you management ideas based on an overall concept of social media.

I want to help you develop a full understanding of how you can use Web 2.0 as a set of tools and services.

Please send any comments about this tweet-book to my Twitter account, @jucarjim, or to jucar@cograf.com. Thank you!

Juan Carlos Jimenez
April, 2011

Why a book written in tweets?

To write more effective messages, I took two key considerations into account.

First: The written phrases that are easiest to understand have between 15 and 20 words.

A sentence of 15-20 words is long enough to communicate a simple, specific idea.

You can read a sentence of 15-20 words without loosing your train of thought or feeling like you're going to run out of breath.

Reading in rhythm to your breathing helps you concentrate on the message.

If you're more focused on the material, it's much more likely that you'll understand it.

Second: Long sentences are a common fault in written communications.

When we write like we speak, we tend to write very long sentences.

It's easier to follow a verbal conversation, even if there are a lot of "annotations."

But these same verbal "footnotes" in written communications tend to distract and confuse the reader.

In general, it's harder to write correctly and fluently if you do it exactly how you speak.

Verbal communication is full of gestures and inflections that are hard to convey in writing.

To express pauses and emphasis in writing, you would need to have a complete mastery of punctuation.

It requires a lot of practice to write communications in everyday language, which are grammatically correct at the same time.

In this sense, Web 2.0 also gives you the opportunity to practice your written communication skills.

For me, Twitter is like a gym, where I can train for specific, direct and intelligible writing.

When I write a tweet, I always look for ways to make it shorter and more precise.

Remove everything you can from a sentence without losing the meaning: it'll come out better.

When I re-tweet something someone else has written, I also look for ways to make it shorter.

William Shakespeare said, "Brevity is the soul of wit."

Spanish writer, Baltasar García, put it this way: "Something good, if it's brief, is twice as good."

Many good tweets resemble good journalism.

It's very useful for managers to develop a certain journalistic style in commercial or institutional written communications.

Good journalism is direct and focused on the facts. The same is true of good advertising.

In Twitter, you can write a tweet of up to 140 characters, but if you want other people to re-tweet it, you should use only 120 to 130.

By not using the full 140 characters, you enable others to add comments to your tweets and converse with you.

If you practice your written communication in Twitter, your messages in other media will improve immediately.

Twitter can help you with all of your commercial or institutional written communications.

In Twitter, you can easily try out different ways of expressing an idea for free.

Present the same idea in different ways and see which one draws more attention.

You may discover that many of your marketing messages draw more attention when they're questions instead of statements.

You may discover that the web surfer's responses make better publicity than your messages.

Also, with innumerable references posted by its users, Twitter is a great source of learning and inspiration.

There's much to be learned from reading and enjoying the way other people write.

Hopefully, these ideas on how organizations can converse in Web 2.0 will be interesting and useful to you.

Thanks to its size, you can post on Twitter each paragraph in this book that you like most.

Some key terminology

In these topics, you'll always find terms that are used as synonyms: Social Networks, Web 2.0 and "Social Media."

These terms have much in common, but can have different connotations.

The concept of social networks is nothing new. It's part of the history of humankind.

Your social networks are made up of different types of relationships that you have with various groups of people.

You take advantage of these relationships for purposes of entertainment, business, education or even sales.

You're using your social networks when you call your friends or family to offer or ask for help, information, advice and favors.

Each one of these groups of relationships and networks of people you know are your communities.

The durability of the relationships in your communities depends on the intensity of your interaction in them.

From a professional, business or personal perspective, these relationships are also known as relationship capital.

The relationship capital in your social networks functions like a savings account: it gives dividends if you make deposits.

If all you do is ask your friends and family for favors (withdrawals), your relationships are weakened (and accrue little interest).

If you use your social networks only for commercial purposes, this diminishes people's confidence in you.

If you're an entrepreneur or manager, you already know the value of socializing with your team.

As you continue gaining the confidence of your team, you'll create a more harmonious and productive workplace.

If you want your employees to feel more identified with their work, you must expand your relationships with them.

If all you do is give orders to your workers without listening to them or taking their ideas into account, you won't have a very good relationship with them.

Your interaction with your family members is just as important. More respect leads to more unity.

True respect requires closeness in order to better acknowledge and listen to the other person.

People who respect and acknowledge each other can communicate better and form stronger relationships.

As you can see, the concept of social networks has always existed in your life.

One way or another, some more than others, we all share in the social networks we have.

Socializing is one of the key signs of an increasingly interconnected, interrelated and "Internet-ted" world.

People socialize more because they have more means and more necessity to do so.

With Web 2.0, people can rely on a huge number of tools and resources for conversing more easily.

Social networks on the Internet

The concept of social networks in this book has two con-notations: virtual communities and interaction tools.

Virtual communities on the Internet consist of your own network of direct relationships and their networks of relationships.

Direct relationships

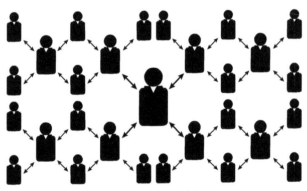

Indirect relationships

It's the interrelation of different networks that gives so much power to social networks.

They've always been influential, but with the Internet, the power of social networks is greater.

You know that satisfied clients speak well of your business in their communities and direct relationships.

The power of multiplication of a message in social networks is what's always been known as word-of-mouth.

The power of word-of-mouth advertising: people are more likely to try products recommended by their friends.

People believe and trust the people they have relationships with, because they've already tried that service or product.

People turn to their social networks to ask advice on products and services.

Many people all over the world use social networks as tools for expressing their opinions on products and services.

To understand how to take advantage of the communi-cational power of Web 2.0, you must view it as a tool.

Social networks on the Internet function thanks to certain website's free services, which stimulate personal interaction.

The easier it is to interact in 2.0 sites, the more quickly virtual communities are formed in them.

For a commercial or social organization, social networks make extraordinary platforms for communication and providing information.

2.0 services and tools are useful for external and internal communications in an organization.

On the inside, businesses are networks of relationships and their various departments are communities.

Regardless of their number, if people are interacting, there's a community conversing.

Wherever there's conversation, Web 2.0 has the potential to make it easier, stronger and more extensive.

However, like any tool, the effectiveness of networks (as a means of communication) depends on how they're used.

Web 2.0

The term "Web 2.0" was used for the first time in 2004 by the publisher, O'Reilly Media, specializing in IT.

They wanted to differentiate it from Web 1.0, where the content didn't allow for the active participation of web surfers.

1.0 websites are typically those of companies and institutions, with one-way communications.

The management mentality of 1.0 is based on the desire to control what is published.

The media (TV, radio and print) are also 1.0. They do not enable any kind of public interaction.

However, many media websites have evolved and, today, take an active part in the world of 2.0.

Among the first notable 2.0 websites were blogs, a service that became popular in 2000.

The technology of blogs democratized the possibility of creating content and sharing it with the world.

Thanks to blogs, unknown individuals began to exert a great influence on public opinion within a short period of time.

Blogs encouraged communities that shared their experiences in specific areas of common interest.

The fact that blogs were free, easy to use and highly interactive ensured their place as the most popular Web 2.0 sites.

Blogs function as socialization tools that stimulate the formation of social networks.

Before blogs, the main platform of social networks on the Internet was email and its web-based variants.

Afterwards, sites emerged that opened up the possibility for people to create their own groups of friends and followers within specific topics.

In 2002, Friendster appeared, followed by MySpace in 2003, Facebook in 2004 and Twitter in 2006.

Over the ensuing years, thousands of additional dialogue 2.0 services have appeared.

A few Web 2.0 services

As you have noticed, the terms "Web 2.0," "social media" and "social networks" can be used as synonyms.

Web 2.0 refers to types of websites based on certain technologies and content geared toward encouraging participation.

Social media encompass a variety of web services that enable virtual and digital socialization (text, photos, voice and video).

Social networks are a consequence of benefiting from the use of Web 2.0 for various purposes (commercial, entertainment, etc.).

If you view Web 2.0 as an integrated group of socialization media, you'll be able to interact more effectively in the existing communities.

If you converse effectively, you'll be able to create your own conversations and communities of followers.

Remember that you must present topics of common interest in order to draw attention and motivate interaction.

If your Web 2.0 messages are only promotional, you'll motivate rejection.

Matters of customer service and practical advice can be managed through Facebook and Twitter.

For business topics that you need to address in more detail, you can turn to a blog.

In Blogger.com, WordPress.com or Tumblr.com, you can configure your blog quickly at no cost.

If you're interested in publishing photos of your products, services or facilities, use services like Flickr.com or Sonico.com.

You can post videos related to your activities on YouTube.com or Vimeo.com, even from your cell phone.

You can distribute corporate documents or presentations through services like SlideShare.com or Scribd.com.

There are interesting services available, like TwtVite.com, where you can send out 2.0 invitations to events or promotions.

You can also take surveys with ease, using free services like TwtPoll.com.

A respected tool for posting your professional profile and resume is Linkedin.com.

Your organization's news can reach a larger audience through services like Digg.com or Meneame.com.

There are also free tools for tracking your presence in Web 2.0, like SocialMention.com or HowSociable.com.

You can take advantage of all of these services as much more than simply promotional platforms for your activities.

You can also benefit from 2.0 services as management and conversation tools within your organization.

The value to your organization

Your current and potential clients are already in the social networks, talking about many things, including products and services.

In Web 2.0, people talk about their experiences with major brands and small businesses, alike.

You can't find out what they're saying if you don't participate, even if only in a conservative way.

If neither you nor your business has a presence in virtual communities, you're giving your competitors an advantage.

Social networks allow you to find out which topics are most important to people, as well as people's greatest concerns.

Through the various conversations in 2.0 communities, you can discover people's unsatisfied needs.

Knowing and understanding people's expectations forms a basis for identifying business opportunities.

Finding your market through social networks is less expensive than using other methods.

The people on your work team also converse in social networks.

If you involve them effectively, your employees can be spokespersons and representatives for your activities.

Some companies have been training their personnel to provide customer service in virtual communities.

Preparing workers to participate in social networks multiplies an organization's customer service channels.

The company, Best Buy, has more than 2,300 employees advising and responding to customers through Twitter.

If your people feel like part of the company culture, they'll talk about being part of it with pride in the social networks.

Through the participation of their workers in social networks, companies can attract more human resources.

Other organizations take advantage of certain social network services to support their management and operations.

There are work teams that communicate with each other more effectively through social media than through email.

Others have improved their document distribution through sites like Scribd.com.

Sharing digital files through 2.0 services reduces traffic on many companies' internal networks.

Other organizations are taking advantage of virtual communities to do market research.

In 2009, the company, Starbucks, obtained more than 100,000 ideas from their customers on how to boost their business.

Dialogue 2.0 with external and internal customers can be a less expensive way to generate significant brand loyalty.

The amount of money your organization can save with Web 2.0, in terms of management and communication, is enormous.

The value of the relationship capital that you can build in social networks can also be very high.

Keep in mind that you can use the basic services in all of the social networks for free.

There's no comparison between that and the cost of developing these services yourself for the exclusive use of your business.

Likewise, some social networks offer more advanced services at a much lower cost than providing them "in-house."

You'll learn more about how you can take advantage of social networks by participating in them than by being too shy to participate.

In terms of image, you risk more by not participating in social networks than by participating.

Like almost anything else of value, trust and credibility are not gained overnight.

It isn't hard to converse in Web 2.0 and gain management benefits, but you need more mental-management flexibility.

How a business should communicate

Sharing is one of the key signs of an increasingly inter-connected, interrelated and "Internet-ted" society.

People communicate and socialize more each day because they have a greater need and more ways to do so.

Socializing satisfies the human need to feel like part of a group where we can share our interests.

When socializing, all topics are important, whether serious or mundane, sacred or profane.

The importance of the topics we share is determined by the needs of each person.

"Public Relations" are a form of socializing, but they don't work the same way in social networks.

Public relations always take a "serious" approach. They don't usually leave room for anything that isn't "institutional."

Many companies don't see the value of socializing, because they think it is something not directly related to their business.

If you fail to see the relevance of socializing for your company, you tend to see the things people say in Web 2.0 as trivial.

The trivialities that people talk about in social media aren't relevant; what's relevant is that now people can do that.

People also talk about products, services, companies, projects, news, politics, etc. in the social networks.

Currently, many Web 2.0 sites have greater power over public opinion than TV, radio, newspapers and magazines.

Traditional mass media have been superseded by the reach and immediacy of Web 2.0.

Social networks have made it easier for people to experience their collective power of influence simply by socialWith Web 2.0, not only companies and institutions are globalized, but also regular, everyday people.

Publicly sharing ideas and feelings is a social aspiration that Web 2.0 helps satisfy.

The platform of social networks does a good deal to help people reaffirm their identity within their groups of interest.

Finding people with common interests in different parts of the world reaffirms our humanity in one way or another.

Socializing is one of the basic human needs: we are outgoing.

If you fail to understand that this is a need, it'll be hard for you to understand the value of socializing for your business.

For entrepreneurs and managers, the concept of socializing in Web 2.0 is, perhaps, the hardest part to digest.

Public relations and social-company responsibility are limited approaches in social networks.

Socializing in virtual communities makes it necessary for each company to find a way of being a person, as well as an organization.

Being a person isn't a common idea in business, most of all if you have put a lot of effort into creating institutionalism.

It's easier for companies to see themselves as a person when they're closer to consumers.

A company is a person when it treats each customer as an individual instead of just another client.

Companies and institutions act as people when they treat clients as human beings and not just end-users.

Being a person in social networks necessitates understanding that sometimes you have to be more informal with your contacts.

You must learn when it's more appropriate to be formal or informal in social networks.

In order to socialize authentically, companies must be more humble and flexible.

There's no recipe for how a company socializes in the social networks. Each company must do it based on its objectives.

Socializing also depends on the "fame" of each company. Well-known companies have more "natural" influence.

Famous companies and people already have a lot of followers and "friends" who talk about them.

Famous people and companies face different challenges in socializing from those faced by unknowns.

Famous brands have more exposure in social networks because they have an impact on many people's lives.

If your company isn't famous, you must converse more in social media, but you also have more agility than large companies.

Small companies have much less bureaucracy than large ones. This gives them more speed when socializing.

It's worth mentioning that having a lot of followers in social networks isn't necessarily the same thing as socializing.

Many famous companies and people hardly interact with their followers and follow very few people.

A company that socializes in Web 2.0 doesn't have a profile simply for handing customer complaints and claims.

The worst way for a company to converse in social networks is to devote itself mainly to self-promotion.

A company that truly socializes in Web 2.0 also follows many people, interacts with them and recommends them.

Socializing in social networks is much more than simply gaining followers...

If you get a new follower in a social network, don't automatically assume that it's a fan.

Socializing in Web 2.0 as a company is your way and means of relating to people, above and beyond your commercial mission.

When a social or commercial organization truly converses in Web 2.0, there's more give and take.

To socialize in Web 2.0 as a company or manager, you must assume an equitable relationship in the virtual communities.

Companies need an increased sense of humility in order to effectively socialize in social networks.

If you're humble enough to learn, your business has much to gain from Web 2.0.

Companies learn to converse in social networks when they place more emphasis on listening.

Begin the dialogue by listening

Listening is the first principle you must apply in order to derive communicational benefits from dialogue 2.0.

For companies, listening isn't an obvious strategy. Historically, advertising has always been one-way.

The companies that find more and better business opportunities are those that develop empathetic listening skills in the market.

In Web 2.0, listening empathetically is one of the fundamental keys to corporate communication, marketing and advertising.

Your company needs to open its ears. Listen well and listen to everything. Listen to understand and to learn.

No matter what type of business you're in, listening in the social networks involves reading between the lines with empathy.

Listen to everything: the good, the bad and everything in-between, and apply the principles of comprehensive reading.

Comprehensive reading means meeting more people, discovering what they think and learning in the process.

When listening, your main goal as a business is to try to understand the thoughts and feelings in your market.

Understanding aspirations of your public and their origin forms the basis for your opportunities in the immediate future.

Listen with humility to what they say about your brand, your company, your products, your industry and your competitors.

If you don't listen with humility, all you'll hear are words without meaning, and you'll miss the reasons behind them.

Companies that listen with humility in Web 2.0 do so without prejudice. They don't just pretend to listen.

When companies listen with humility show a basic gesture of respect, which is expected in virtual communities.

If your company doesn't listen patiently, without arrogance, it won't be able to really tune in to the social media.

Listening with humility allows you see opportunities for improvement. Otherwise, all you hear will be frivolity or provocation.

Remember, clients become fans of those who are careful to listen and understand them.

Clients have always believed and trusted more in those companies that listen to them the most.

When a company listens to its customers empathetically, this demonstrates acknowledgment, respect and appreciation.

Listening (reading with empathy) enables companies to provide good customer service in social media.

Companies can also benefit from social networks when they listen to what isn't being said about them.

Researching and following the key topics for your company are reason enough to exercise your ears in virtual communities.

Many companies don't have a Web 2.0 presence for fear of what they might hear or they believe that it's very difficult to manage.

Listening to 2.0 conversations presents a great opportunity for your organization to improve its customer service.

The companies that listen most in social networks learn more and are more innovative.

The companies that understand that customer complaints are valuable can be more creative, while spending less money.

Companies that encourage and listen to suggestions in social networks reap countless business opportunities.

Don't worry if you don't like what you hear. On the Internet, it's easy to find a certain amount of negativity.

However, negativity in social networks is only part of what these virtual spaces for expression have to offer.

In Web 2.0, people feel that they can express complaints and opinions that companies don't hear through other media.

Customers feel disrespected by companies that don't listen to them. This is why they vent in social networks.

Web 2.0 provides a means for people's free expression, without the limitations of traditional communication media.

Web surfers feel that, in the social media, they have as much or more power than companies to express their opinions.

Web surfers experience their power in social networks every minute of every day.

Companies can save a lot of time and money if they learn to listen respectfully to virtual communities.

The companies that respect virtual communities treat them with a clear sense of equality.

Web surfers experience their power in Web 2.0 through the echo and impact that their opinions can have.

Echoes in social networks include followers, friends, visitors, recommendations, mentions, re-tweets, stars, etc.

When listening, companies must learn to interpret the echoes of various topics that are of interest to them.

Messages about companies in social networks may or may not be direct. To recognize them, you must learn to listen.

Listen to complaints as if you were doing "live" market research. They're a free source of opportunities for improvement.

Remember that customer complaints have always existed; they didn't originate with social networks.

Just because your company doesn't participate in social networks, that doesn't make those complaints go away.

Listening presents a challenge to the maturity of your organization and its corporate reactions.

The way you listen in social networks reflects how much you truly value your customers.

Intelligent listening in Web 2.0 enables them to take care of their customers in a special and memorable way.

Social networks are used by each web surfer in an individual and personal way.

In the social networks, your contacts expect to be heard and taken care of one at a time.

Giving people individual attention is one of the pillars of a good business reputation in social networks.

Listening (reading) empathetically means putting yourself in the other person's shoes. Don't read to judge, but to learn.

Empathetic reading enables you to identify opportunities for your organization that may not be apparent right now.

Reading empathetically in social networks represents a minimal investment with high returns in market intelligence.

The comments of virtual communities can help you improve your products and services.

Listening more and discovering the reasons behind what you hear enables you to have a more interesting 2.0 dialogue.

Certain famous people and companies have a lot of followers, but they follow very few others: they don't listen to them.

If your company only follows a few people, you lose out on the opportunities presented by a diversity of opinions.

Follow people who are beyond the scope of your business. Take advantage of the opportunity to listen to different people.

The more interesting people you follow (and listen to), the better your interconnections will be.

Listening carefully and thoroughly will enable you to "talk" better in Web 2.0.

Guidelines for "talking"

The main difficulty for companies in benefiting from Web 2.0 lies in their inability to converse beyond simply advertising.

Companies need a better understanding of what it means to converse in Web 2.0, a seemingly simple concept.

Conversing isn't that simple, especially for commercial organizations. Their sales paradigms are of no use.

Because of their commercial nature, it's more "natural" for companies to advertise than to converse.

It's easy for people to believe that companies aren't interested in conversing unless it's about business.

If a company only talks about its business, its conversations in social networks will be very boring.

Selling or promoting themselves is what companies like best and practice with ease.

Someone who only talks, and listening very little, is not conversing. This fault is even more noticeable in companies.

When you're used to being very active when speaking, it's easy to lose your sensibility for listening and conversing.

It's understandable that we're more anxious to talk because it makes us feel like we have more power and control.

The most common practices in commercial marketing and advertising are one-way communication and direct sales.

One-way advertising is usually at odds with the conversational tone that people adopt in social networks.

If you only talk about your company or products in Web 2.0, you'll be ignored for being egocentric.

Conversing effectively in the social media involves a lot maturity on the part of the company ego.

For some companies, conversation seems counter-indicated because it doesn't appear to have a clear commercial purpose.

Conversing authentically forms the main basis for companies' success in social networks.

No company will say that conversation isn't fundamental. However, in practice, they aren't very conversational.

Companies have more experience with advertising messages and promotions geared toward short-term results.

Conversing in Web 2.0 doesn't mean devoting yourself to telling everyone how great your company and products are.

Companies must understand that conversations in social networks are like chats among friends.

A dialogue between friends is fresh, varied and light, and deals with various aspects of everyday life.

If friends spoke to each other the way companies usually do, the conversations would be annoying.

Companies tend to converse with messages where they're always trying to sell something.

Always wanting to sell something isn't a bad thing. It's what a company is supposed to do.

The bad thing about companies always selling is that their method and timing might not be appropriate in Web 2.0.

If most of a company's posts are sales messages, it's difficult to truly converse without being "invasive."

To socialize in social networks, companies must take part in the web surfers' conversation.

To take part in dialogue 2.0, companies must effectively support what others say.

If your company can't talk about a topic that goes beyond its business, it's very difficult to have a successful conversation.

Your company must participate in social networks by recommending what other people and organizations say.

Supporting the messages of others with common interests helps your company to be perceived as a noble organization.

Reacting by commenting on what other people say is a way of turning your company into a person.

Conversing also entails giving useful advice to people, whether they're customers or not.

Dialogue 2.0 involves giving guidance to people, even if it benefits your competitors.

Conversing is revealing information that is useful to the general public, not just about your business.

The company must answer legitimate questions in social networks, but in the spirit of service, not defensively.

Don't stress out if you make mistakes. "To err is human". In a conversation between friends, sometimes people say the wrong thing.

If you make a mistake, apologize. Fix it right away and get past it. It's normal in any conversation.

Don't lie: Don't create fake followers, fake profiles or fake votes. You'll always be caught and it'll jeopardize your image.

Don't deny your mistakes right off the bat. Thank people for letting you know and offer to investigate and resolve it.

Acknowledging mistakes quickly is honorable and inspires trust. Honesty is highly-valued in social networks.

Don't torture yourself by responding directly to everything that others say. Conversation also means investigating.

Respond to criticism by offering means of direct contact to provide higher-quality service.

Personalized attention to complaints and criticism helps build trust and credibility.

If you're faced with unjustified messages, don't despair. Sometimes the best response is silence.

Unjustified or senseless messages usually discredit themselves on their own. Don't get into confrontations.

Don't post anything in Web 2.0 that you might later regret.

If you regret something you posted in Web 2.0, you can always delete it. Do it!

Avoid writing out of anger or arrogance. More than a few people could be offended.

"Bitter" written messages could be interpreted as aggression toward people for whom it isn't intended.

If you want to build a good reputation for your business, write in a positive and optimistic spirit.

The company needs to converse like a person and not like a marketing or sales department.

Companies must learn to ask questions in order to truly understand the real needs of people.

Asking questions is the most important marketing activity that a commercial or social organization can undertake.

Organizations that are in the habit of asking questions identify more opportunities for improvement in a more cost-effective way.

In social networks, your company has the opportunity to be a person and socialize as such.

In its communications, your company must think the way a person would in any conversation.

A company is a person when it welcomes and thanks its new followers in social networks.

Companies are also people when they thank their followers for their recommendations and comments.

2.0 dialogues are individual and personal, which is why direct advertising is usually inappropriate.

If you converse in social networks only as an impatient salesperson, your messages will be boring.

For your direct advertising to be heard in Web 2.0, you must first build trust.

Building trust in any social network always takes time and effort, especially for companies.

For people to pay attention to your offers for products and services, you must build up a base of quality followers.

The quality of followers in social networks is determined by the influence they have over others.

Conversing in social networks doesn't mean that companies abandon their current marketing and sales plans.

Conversing in social networks means that companies need another strategy for these virtual communities.

A conversation strategy for social networks doesn't completely exclude direct sales.

For direct sales to be effective in Web 2.0, your organization must build a lot of trust and a good reputation.

The use of 2.0 tools involves targeting promotional messages to very small and specific audiences.

The more specific the message, the more opportunities you'll have to spread it.

To converse effectively in the social media, you need to see the big picture with regard to the role of all communications.

Dialogue 2.0 also challenges you to promote a culture of participation within the organization.

For a company to succeed in social networks requires the participation of its employees.

Improving communication within the work team results in improving their integration and productivity.

Improving communication between employees improves their teamwork and strengthens their commitment to the company.

Web 2.0 also provides an opportunity to develop an organizational culture based on trust.

Conversing in social networks presents an opportunity for your company to learn to be more human.

Modern society has a greater appreciation of organizations that are more human.

Suggested outline for your plan

I imagine that if you've read this far, it's because you're interested in knowing how to put these ideas into practice.

Each person has his or her own necessities. So, you should adapt this plan outline to your situation.

It isn't a recipe or a set of inflexible guidelines. It's simply 5 practical criteria that will give you a place to start.

I have already given you some of the ideas in this plan outline, but here they are in a structured format.

It's a simple plan, directed toward owners or managers of commercial or social organizations, like you.

This plan doesn't require expertise in technology; all you need to know how to do is use the Internet.

Since it's just a minimal start-up plan, the only investment you need to make is 15 minutes of your time each day.

1. It's like a marathon rather than a 100-yard dash. The key is perseverance and endurance, not speed.

You need to aim far. This will give you a better shot.

Don't expect instant popularity as soon as you create a profile in Twitter or Facebook or start a blog.

Only personalities and brands that were famous before participating in Web 2.0 get followers easily.

A good reputation in social networks takes perseverance, creativity, discipline and time.

Keep in mind that, in social networks, the governing principle is that quality counts more than quantityLearning how to socialize productively as a company and entrepreneur won't happen overnight.

Marathon's vision will help you better define your goals and understand that your efforts has to be gradual.

Involve your employees in the process of learning how to converse in Web 2.0.

2. Have clear objectives, both for yourself, as a person, entrepreneur and manager, and for your business.

Having clear objectives related to Web 2.0 will enable you to understand the requirements better and formulate a work plan.

The resources and effort you will have to invest will be in direct proportion to how ambitious your objectives are.

Here are a few medium-term business objectives that you can adapt to your specific case:

- To **learn** about the implications of dialogue 2.0, as a company and as an entrepreneur.

- To better **understand** what your current or potential clients think and feel and how they express it.

- To **advise** the participants in these virtual communities on topics related to your business.

- To **promote** your products, services and projects to create new opportunities.

- To **develop** an organizational culture that promotes trust and productive dialogue.

3. Start as soon as possible. The best way to learn is by doing.

As an entrepreneur, publish at least one personal profile in the social networks, and another one for your business.

Two profiles will help you participate in Web 2.0, according to the specific interests in each case.

You could also publish a profile for your "star" product or service.

Publishing your profiles in Web 2.0 enables you to learn about available names and about your competitors.

Publishing profiles is the first step to participating in the various social networks that are of value to you.

It's a good idea to have a profile photo that corresponds to the way you want to be identified as a person or company.

Involve your work team in your 2.0 strategy and decision making processes. That way, you'll encourage greater commitment.

4. Be yourself, but remember: you represent the brand of your business, project, product, service or organization.

2.0 communities aren't an abstract bunch of consumers, clients or prospects. First and foremost, they're people.

People in social networks want to interact and share with other people who have their own feelings and opinions.

Web surfers prefer to converse with organizations that act more like people than inflexible machines.

A style of communication that is always formal or like letter-writing doesn't work in social networks.

If you're capable of listening and understanding, rather than acting like a robot, your company will be perceived as human.

As a company, you must demonstrate social interests in Web 2.0 that go beyond your business.

Present yourself as a person and a company that can make human connections with others, beyond your commercial objectives.

5. Employ the guidelines for listening and talking in Web 2.0 that I gave you earlier.

Start following others and recommend what they say on topics related to your interests and those of your company.

Virtual communities revolve around topics, so you must post your messages in those same terms.

Find out what people say about topics of interest to you and your business in the corresponding social networking sites.

The thematic vision of dialogue 2.0 will help you identify valuable contacts that you haven't met yet.

To begin establishing an interesting Web 2.0 presence, you only have to invest about 15 minutes a day.

When posting messages, find the balance: 1/3 about you, 1/3 for recommending ideas and news items and 1/3 for conversation.

Each Web 2.0 site requires a different type of effort, where the most important thing is quality and not quantity.

Researching and reading what people think is also a way of socializing in Web 2.0.

Recommended reading

Here are a few publications and websites that may be of interest to you if you would like to learn more about related topics:

BACON, Jono (2009). *The Art of Community*. O'Reilly Media. http://www.artofcommunityonline.org

BROGAN, Chris (2008). *Social Media and Social Networking Starting Points*. http://www.chrisbrogan.com

JANTSCH, John (). Let's talk. *Social Media for Small Business*. http://www.ducttapemarketing.com/socialmediaforbusiness.pdf

JIMENEZ, Juan Carlos (2008). *Email at the workplace: A Survival Guide. Solutions and tips* (In English). Available at Amazon.com.

MAYFIELD, Antony (2008) *What Is Social Media?. An e-book by from iCrossing.*
http://www.icrossing.co.uk/ebooks

MEERMAN SCOTT, David (2008). *The New Rules of Viral Marketing. How word-of-mouse spreads your ideas for free.*
http://www.davidmeermanscott.com

NASLUND, Amber (2009). *The Social Media Starter Kit.*
http://bit.ly/m8aNtS

SOLIS, Brian (2008). *The Essential Guide to Social Media.*
http://www.briansolis.com

SOLIS, Brian (2009). *Customer Service: The Art of Listening and Engagement Through Social Media.*
http://www.briansolis.com

About the author

Juan Carlos Jimenez began his professional career in 1978 as a graphic designer. He has worked as a Creative Director in publishing companies, printed communications media, design studios and advertising agencies.

In 1990, he founded Cograf Comunicaciones, where he works in the areas of brand identity project design and execution, corporate communications, marketing, sales, Internet and customer service.

He develops professional advice and training programs to promote a culture of customer service and high-performance work teams, based on values of personal excellence.

Since 1996, he has shared his ideas on how managers can benefit from the Internet in www.internetips.com. Along the same lines, he wrote the books, "Negocios.com," "Mercadeo.com" and "E-mail at the workplace."

He has also contributed to the professional development of people and companies through other books: "The significance of values in an organization," "Increase your opportunities", "Supreme Art" and " "Learn with efficiency".

He has been an invited professor at various universities in Venezuela, giving lectures on marketing, strategic communications and the Internet.

He continuously shares his ideas and recommendations in numerous seminars, conferences and corporate events throughout Venezuela and other countries where he has been an invited speaker.

Cograf Inc. Books

The Significance of Values in an organization

Increase your opportunities. Paradigms for personal motivation

Supreme Art: 50 good customer service practices

Email at the workplace: A Survival Guide. Solutions and tips

Aprende con eficacia [Learn with efficiency: Improve your assimilation and retention]

Mercadeo.com [Practical pointers on image, marketing and sales for entrepreneurs and managers]

www.cografin.com

Cograf Inc

We provide support for companies and social organizations to internally promote values related to individual responsibility, personal excellence, customer service, interpersonal communication, teamwork, a vision of the future and change management.

We offer conferences, seminars, workshops, training programs, management coaching, corporate events and special meetings on these topics, adapted to our clients' needs and situations.

If you would like to obtain extra copies of our books to distribute them in your company or among your friends and colleagues, we offer unique volume discounts.

We also produce special editions of these books with your company's logo on the cover and a special message for your organization, signed by your directors or representatives.

Contact us:
E-mail: jucar@cografinc.com
www.cografinc.com

www.cografinc.com

www.cograf.com

www.cursoscograf.com

www.libroscograf.com

www.internetips.com

www.folletoweb.com

cograf.wordpress.com

www.facebook.com/cograf

www.dialogo2punto0.com

www.artesupremo.com

www.ampliatusoportunidades.com

www.elvalordelosvalores.com

www.dialogo2punto0.com